MW01170775

FROM MY HEART

Poems from the Desert to New Life

Valencia Davis

FROM MY HEART

Poems from the Desert to New Life

Copyright © 2024 by Valencia Davis.

All rights reserved. No part of this book may be reproduced or transmitted in any form or by any means without written permission from the author.

ISBN: 979-8-9894463-3-9

Build A Brother Publishing

DEDICATION

For all the soldiers who have ever served in the military whether on the front line or in the rear, on the battlefield overseas or at home. For all those still serving, try to remember that the battle is not yours, it belongs to the Lord and He has already won the victory for you.

Thank you to everyone who reads my poems. My faith has been tried and tested many times. There is a saying that "what doesn't kill you makes you stronger." My experiences in life - in the desert, the mountains, and the valleys, dodging bullets and bombs, and even fighting cancer - all have brought me to the place I am now. I am still standing strong, and holding on to my faith. I dedicate this book to those of you who choose to do the same.

"No matter what happens, or how bad it seems today,
life goes on, and it will be better tomorrow."

MAYA ANGELOU

FOREWARD

By Carlos Malone Sr.

In the realm of artistic expression, where words are both the brush and the palette, the significance of passion and an unwavering dedication to one's craft cannot be overstated. It is this very ethos that Valencia Davis embodies in her remarkable poetry collection, *From My Heart*. Her work is not just a testament to her skill as a writer but a beacon for all who believe in the transformative power of art.

The journey of an artist is often solitary, traversing through the landscapes of the soul in search of truths that resonate with the universal human experience. Valencia's odyssey, however, takes a path less trodden. In the desolate yet poignant backdrop of Afghanistan amidst warfare, she discovered a sanctuary of serenity within herself. Amid the cacophony of conflict, Valencia found her voice—a voice that is both tender and powerful, capable of weaving tranquility from turmoil.

From My Heart emerges not just as a collection of poems but as a pilgrimage through the human spirit. Valencia's words are imbued with the authenticity of someone who has peered into the abyss and found within it a wellspring of inspiration. Her ability to capture the ephemeral beauty of life, even in its darkest moments, is nothing short of miraculous.

This book is a vessel of real-life experiences, transformed into art through Valencia's unwavering passion and her heartfelt commitment to storytelling. It is a privilege to introduce *From My Heart* to you, the reader, as you embark on this journey alongside her. As you turn each page, let yourself be transported into Valencia's world, where poetry serves as both refuge and revelation.

I extend my deepest commendation to my spiritual daughter, Valencia Davis, for her outstanding achievement. This published work is a gift to us all, a reminder of the power of words to heal, inspire, and transform. Your heart is sure to be deeply moved as you immerse yourself in the narrative she has so eloquently penned.

Welcome to *From My Heart*. May this collection bless you, stir you, and ultimately, connect you more deeply with the wellspring of your own emotions and experiences. Valencia's journey underscores a profound truth: even in the most unlikely places, amidst chaos and desolation, the human spirit can find beauty and peace. Let her words guide you to those quiet places within, where the poetry of life awaits.

PSALM 91

(King James Version)

1. He that dwelleth in the secret place of the most High shall abide under the shadow of the Almighty.

2. I will say of the Lord, He is my refuge and my fortress: my God; in him will I trust.

3. Surely he shall deliver thee from the snare of the fowler, and from the noisome pestilence.

4. He shall cover thee with his feathers, and under his wings shalt thou trust: his truth shall be thy shield and buckler.

5. Thou shalt not be afraid for the terror by night; nor for the arrow that flieth by day;

6. Nor for the pestilence that walketh in darkness; nor for the destruction that wasteth at noonday.

7. A thousand shall fall at thy side, and ten thousand at thy right hand; but it shall not come nigh thee.

8. Only with thine eyes shalt thou behold and see the reward of the wicked.

9. Because thou hast made the Lord, which is my refuge, even the most High, thy habitation;

10. There shall no evil befall thee, neither shall any plague come nigh thy dwelling.

11. For he shall give his angels charge over thee, to keep thee in all thy ways.

12. They shall bear thee up in their hands, lest thou dash thy foot against a stone.

13. Thou shalt tread upon the lion and adder: the young lion and the dragon shalt thou trample under feet.

14. Because he hath set his love upon me, therefore will I deliver him: I will set him on high, because he hath known my name.

15. He shall call upon me, and I will answer him: I will be with him in trouble; I will deliver him, and honour him.

16. With long life will I satisfy him, and shew him my salvation.

TABLE OF CONTENTS

SECTION 1

Answer The Call

Answer The Call

Penning the thoughts
Of my mind onto the paper.
Extricating myself to be
Truly free in
Releasing my inner
Yearnings.

The Summon of the Soul

In stillness deep, where whispers dwell,
A call resounds, not loud but clear,
It stirs the soul, breaks every shell,
To serve, to love, without fear.

No grand stage, nor bright spotlight,
Just hearts to heal, hands to hold,
In humble acts, in kindness bright,
A story of service, silently told.

To answer this call, a journey begins,
Where self is lost, and purpose found,
In service to others, the spirit wins,
In every gesture, His love resounds.

Hibernation

The time is now; the day is here.
I have come to the end of my sleep.
Procrastination is over.
The pages in the book awaits my words.

The Herald's Voice

Upon the wind, a voice does carry,
A call to arms, for those who tarry,
Not of war, but peace to marry,
To the Lord's work, we must not parry.

Fields ripe, in harvest wait,
For willing hearts, to navigate,
The path of service, to dedicate,
Their lives to love, to elevate.

So heed the call, let not it fall,
Upon deaf ears, or hearts so small,
For in His service, we find our all,
And in answering, we stand tall.

Available, But Not Accessible

God's word is both available and accessible.
God's love is accessible; but you have to be available to receive it.
Access is being granted the ability to get what you need.
You cannot access what is not available to you.

Beacon of Hope

A beacon shines, in darkest night,
Guiding the lost, to the light,
A call to serve, to fight the good fight,
To lift the burden, to make the wrong right.

In whispered prayers, in tears that fall,
In every moment, He calls us all,
To be His hands, to break down walls,
To answer the call, to stand tall.

For service is love, made manifest,
A testament of faith, put to the test,
In answering, we are truly blessed,
In the Lord's service, we find our rest.

It's Time

To
Get Up from procrastination and stagnation.
To
Stir Up all the gifts which you possess inside.
To
Stand Up for what is right in God's eyes.

The Shepherd's Call

The Shepherd calls, His flock to lead,
To green pastures, their souls to feed,
In service, their hearts to heed,
The call to love, in every deed.

To walk in faith, to serve with grace,
To see His face, in every place,
To answer the call, to run the race,
With steadfast pace, His love to embrace.

For in His service, we find our way,
To brighter days, to kneel and pray,
To answer His call, come what may,
In His love to stay, every day.

Distractions

Daily
Insignificant
Strategies of the enemy
That may
Risk you
Actually
Connecting
To what is
Important in
Order that you
Not
Succeed.

Ode to the Servant's Heart

In quiet corners, where light is sparse,
The call to service, in hearts does parse,
A stirring deep, a silent arse,
To live for others, to disperse.

The servant's heart, a rare find,
In selfless love, to all mankind,
To answer the call, to unbind,
The chains of self, to be aligned.

With every act, a prayer in motion,
A living, breathing, devotion,
To serve, to love, with deep emotion,
In answering the call, we find our potion.

Vision vs Focus

Vision is seeing clear.
Focus is when you allow nothing to stop your
vision from coming to life.

I'm not complaining

It could be raining
Lord, Thank You for the sunshine.
There is so much going on
None of it is new
Your word told us of days like this that would come.
We should not be surprised
No need to run for our lives.
You are still in control.
Famines, earthquakes, floods and plagues
Sickness, Diseases, Death and more.
No matter what may show up on the scene
Jesus Christ STILL reigns and HE is KING!!

You Have Not Because You Ask Not

What is it that you want?
Cannot seem to grasp it.
Don't have enough money?
If you could buy it, you'd have it. Possessions.
The things you want are not necessarily the things you need.
Your heavenly father already knows what you have need of. He is rich beyond your imagination.
Just ask and you shall receive.

What If

Tonight your soul was required of you
Would you be ready??
If tonight was your last night on earth to live
What would you do with it?
Would you party till the sun came up?
No, sorry, you don't have the time.
Would you ask the time keeper more hours to give
No man knows the hour or the day today your soul could be required.

You say you love me yes lord you know I do. Then feed my sheep.
You say you love me,
Yes lord, you know I do
Then feed my sheep.
You say you love me
Lord why do you ask me again?
My sheep are going astray and hungry
Feed them and herd them back into the fold.
The little ones who believe parents can do no wrong they soak up
knowledge like it were a sponge.
That teenager who wants so much to be grown
Let them know to take it slow.
The young adult who needs guidance and protection from themselves
And
Don't forget the elderly.

OPEN MY EYES

LORD,
Open my eyes,
Open my ears,
Open my mouth,
Open my heart.

That I may see clearly past the distractions.
That I may hear your still small voice, even in the noise.
That I may speak your truths not man's feelings.
So, that your LOVE is felt.
This is my prayer.

New Year

LORD GOD.
Continue to speak to me.
Show me what you want me to see,
Tell me what you want me to say.
It's all about knowing your way.,
No, I am not a Preacher.
But, we all are called to minister.
To tend to the needs of others.
To show true love towards our sisters and brothers.
AGAPE Love is Easy;
When you follow Christ.

SECTION 2

In The Wilderness

In the open desert

Heat and sun
Mirages appear in our eyesight
It is safe up ahead
Wait
Is that a building, a few people a village maybe
No, just an old donkey cart on the side of the road boom, burst,
Wait.........
Bomb
Too late!
Medic,
Patrol will pick up the pieces.
If any

Dust and Echoes

In lands where dusty whispers blow,
Across the hills, in valleys low,
A soldier marches, face set stern,
Bearing the weight of lessons learned.

Each step a testament to will,
In landscapes that are never still,
The echo of a distant fight,
A journey through the longest night.

The wilderness of heart and mind,
A quest for peace, so hard to find,
In every shadow, every sound,
A reminder of the battleground.

Yet in this desolation, stark,
A flicker in the endless dark,
Hope whispers on the wind's soft breath,
A soldier's creed, in life and death.

Still

Still; today
Why I cry sometimes.
Alone I sit with heavy heart,
From my thoughts I cannot part
The darkness swells up around me
Reminders of the many day and nights
Spent waiting for the next sunrise.
Three years have passed for me since I returned time continues on.
Yet more troops continue to deploy.
But time has stopped for those of us who mourn we say a prayer; we lament
Do we as a nation care what those lives meant?
This was a soldier, fighter - somebody's family member.
Their bodies return by flights in the night.
No fanfare - no parades; basically out of sight.
Why is this dark cloud of secrecy allowed?
They do not want you to know the truth because the truth would set you free. Free from all the hypocrisy.

The Warrior's Solace

Amidst the rugged, arid plains,
Where silence reigns, and vastness spans,
There stands a warrior, alone,
Carving strength from every stone.

The sun, a relentless foe,
Matches the fire in his soul,
Battles waged within his heart,
From external wars set apart.

In solitude, he finds his might,
Underneath the stars, each night,
The wilderness, his harsh mentor,
Teaching resilience, and much more.

His spirit, like the land, endures,
Through every trial that occurs,
In Afghanistan's fierce embrace,
He finds a rugged, solemn grace.

Around the corner

Beyond the forest we don't know what awaits us
With anticipation
Beyond the fog we know it is clear
Thick density we see the sunlight calling through the trees.

Valley of Shadows

In the valley where shadows fall,
And silence answers every call,
A soul wanders, lost, alone,
In a wilderness, not of stone.

Dry season of the heart and mind,
Seeking what they cannot find,
A wellspring in a barren land,
Guidance by a gentle hand.

Yet even in this desolate place,
There lies a subtle, hidden grace,
For in the darkness, faith is found,
And in silence, God's voice sounds.

The soul learns to walk by faith, not sight,
Finding strength in the darkest night,
Though the journey is long and steep,
The Shepherd guides His wandering sheep.

The pigeon coop

This building in which we occupy for our living quarters
Has barred windows and some are cemented shut.
Fans blow to stir the hot air around.
Daybreaks early.
Sometimes the cool breeze blows around 3am before the sun rises.
Pigeons fly in and out to gather nest material and food for their young
whose cries can be heard throughout the day and night.
Dust and sand gathers on the floor as a covering
Why bother to sweep.
Trying to add water to keep the dust down; only makes mud
I call it inhumane living conditions.
It is certainly not what we are accustomed to.
Some sleep on shelves built into the warehouse so they are not close to
the floor.
But I am not complaining. We could be outside with or without a tent.
On the ground. Here we do have a cot, you can use your sleeping bag,
sheets, blankets, whatever you have to make your area comfortable
This is now our home

Desert Bloom

In the heart's desert, wide and bare,
Where hope seems like a rare affair,
A Christian stands, faith put to test,
In the wilderness, they seek their rest.

But even deserts know the rain,
And seasons change, relieve the pain,
From barren ground, life can bloom,
In the most unexpected room.

Through trials, faith grows deep and strong,
In weakness, we are made strong,
The desert teaches to rely,
On the One who hears our every sigh.

So, in this dry and thirsty land,
We learn to trust, and understand,
That even in our driest season,
God works for good, with perfect reason.

Again, last night the mortars fell
Some soldier yelled out what the h-- sirens wail, alarms are sounded
The force it made the building shake
Those almost sleep, now very wide awake.
Roll call is done. Platoons sergeants call your name.
All accounted for, everyone is in place.
Reality check. This is not no game.
Choppers rise into the darkened skies. They search for an enemy long
gone now.
Back into the sleeping bag i go.
For I am not afraid of these terrors by night.
Again, I drift slowly off to sleep with angels watching over me.

Journey Through the Wilderness

Through the wilderness, we all must roam,
Sometimes feeling far from home,
A Christian in a season dry,
Underneath the vast, unending sky.

Yet, this wilderness is not in vain,
For through the struggle, through the pain,
We're shaped, refined, made anew,
Drawn closer to the One who's true.

With every step, the path seems clearer,
With every trial, God draws nearer,
The wilderness, once bleak and vast,
Becomes the ground for faith that lasts.

So, embrace the journey, step by step,
In every moment, closely kept,
For in the wilderness, we find,
A deeper love for humankind.

Interruption

It was time to go eat dinner.
We call it our social hour
We sit, we eat, we laugh, we talk,
It is as close to normal as we get.

Tonight was different. As we prepared to make our move to take the walk
The sound of a missile flying by took hold.
Boom boom boom
The building shook with force, plaster falls get down, get down.
-

- get your helmets on, flak vests too. Form up; roll call for 2nd platoon.
13 present, 1 in class; 1 in tae bo. Everyone is accounted for.
Once again we are safe from the terrors of war.

Baghdad

In this ancient land
The desert sands rise up beneath my boots.
I walk the streets and see the
Devastation and destruction
of
What was once the beginnings of man.
Damascus
Babylon
Mesopotamia
Now Iraq.
The great rivers run through this land.
The Tigris
The Euphrates.

As i walk these ancient lands
The desert sands
Underneath my feet
Are like baby powder fine
Here in
Afghanistan.
The desert rocks of Kuwait.
They are:
Smooth black
Deep brown
Sand white
To me these are the colors of mankind.

Answer the call

From citizen to soldier in a matter of minutes.
All it takes is one telephone call.
My call came to my desk on Monday, March 18, 2002.
Imagine, going from reservist to active duty soldier,
No more weekend warrior, this will now be my full-time job.
Until??????
How long? No-one can say with certainty at this time.
There is so much to do.
Forms to complete. Wills. Powers of attorney, briefings to attend.
What do i tell my husband, my children, my family, friends, and
employer?
Adjust fire. Time to go. Say good-bye.
Board the bus. Report for processing. So much work to be done.
We take the c-17 aircraft across the vast skies and several time zones.
United states, Europe; finally Afghanistan.
Now on ground. 2nd platoon, 834th postal detachment.
Morale boosters, maximize the possibilities. To whom much is given,
much is required. I shall do all things through Christ, who strengthens
me.
We deliver. First class.
Hooah "

Deployment

They say we have to go
We leave home, jobs, spouses, kids. Everything about the lives we lived
is now put on hold.
So that
We may journey off to faraway lands to fight in wars
For political cause.
Young men and women
Some barely
Eighteen years old
Are
Dying on the front lines
Shedding their blood.
For the cause.

FROM MY HEART

My purpose is to make a difference
Why are we here in Baghdad, Iraq
I hear this question asked repeatedly.
I even ask it myself.
It is not to fight a war - the war is over.
We are here to support a cause
Something bigger than us.

Back home

Having been across the world to many places unknown can someone
please explain to me
How do you get back home?
The sights, the sounds, the memories
They are all so real
The bombs, mortars, bullets
You know I could have been killed,
The Taliban, Shiites, Sunni
I had no personal quarrel with them my sworn allegiance is to defend
The constitution of the USA
Three years have passed
The dreams are less
I think I am ok
But
Sometimes I cry; sometimes I think
Why I came back, not them?
How come I came back?
Why did I return?
To this my life
My kids, the job, the church.
I am a wife, mother, sister, and friend
All of that and more.
But
Where am I really
In my mind
Still there with my fellow soldiers.
For those still constantly in harms way the war continues.

Afghan moon

Behold, a crescent moon.
Silhouetted mountain tops, blue-grey night sky.
Aligned with the moon, and two planets turning in unison.
The sky is lit with twinkling stars.
Clearly they are seen in the distance.
Only they light the sky above my tent,
I am miles away from what I know as hope.
Here on foreign soil, things are so different.
Yet
Up above in radiant tranquility;
The crescent moon shines.
Wait.
Behind the mountain top
It disappeared from my sight.
Tomorrow i will search the skies for its beauty.
Please show yourself to me again.
The nightlight to my essence.

Reservist in bagram

Beautiful moon that lights the sky.
One bright star to shine
Windy breezes as if the ocean was nearby.
Sandstorms fly up from the ground at any time.
This is the existence we have for now.
How long our stay - we do not know.
The days are long; the sun rises at 0400 (4am) the nights are long; we
have nowhere to go.
This ancient land, once beautiful. Now scarred from years of war.
The people continue to fight,
For
What we in America call freedom/democracy.
At what cost this freedom they are receiving? We come, we bomb, we
help; we build.
Are we truly helping?
Who can answer this?
Let me know when the answer arrives.
For i am here and i cannot tell you the truth.

SECTION 3

Trust The Process

Allow Me To Apologize

Let me apologize
These feelings are real
The caring, sharing of thoughts unpretentious
Time and circumstances will not allow for actuality of these feelings.
Our reality is that there are conditions: marriage, children, the feelings
of others to consider.
They all outweigh the rushing of the heart and longings of the loins.
I do not apologize for these feelings I have for I am human. What I am
sorry for is that you will never know how deep the radiant currents
flowed within the ventricles of my heart.

In Desert Sands

In desert sands, beneath a foreign sky,
I tread where shadows blend with light.
A soldier, yes, but also I,
A woman fighting through the night.
The bullets whisper past, a deadly song,
Yet in this chaos, I find where I belong.
Each step, a testament to strength and fear,
In Afghanistan, where the lines of life are clear.

Through dust and danger, my heart beats on,
A rhythm set by life's demanding dance.
Here, where day and night are drawn,
I seek not glory, nor do I chance.
But for peace, for home, for those I love,
I stand, beneath the vast, uncaring sky above.

When I first came back,
I wanted to be
The me I used to be.
BUT
Then I began to see
That she was no longer me.
I left her home when I crossed the sea.
Why can't I find her anymore??
That me I used to be.
She has changed along the way.
Egypt, El Salvador, Germany, Afghanistan; finally to Iraq.
Things will never be the same.
NOW
I'm different.
I've changed somehow.
YET
I yearn,
For that me I used to be;
STILL.....

Beyond the Burden

Beyond the burden of the battle's weight,
Where every moment's choice is life or death,
I find a strength, unwavering and great,
Inhaled with every shallow, dusty breath.
Afghanistan's rugged hills bear witness
To the struggle, the pain, the soldier's plight,
Yet in this land of age-old stress,
I've found a purpose, shining bright.

I fight not just for orders from above,
But for the laughter, the tears, the human soul,
For every act of unexpected love,
In a world that's fragmented, yet whole.
Here, in the heart of conflict, I've grown,
A woman soldier, fierce, fully known.

Freedom

Forever
Released and
Externally
Extrapolated from
Demands
Of
Mankind.

The Journey

This journey through the valley, dark and deep,
Where shadows linger and the rivers swell,
Is but a path the faithful choose to keep,
A testament to stories we must tell.
Life's process, a pilgrimage of sorts,
With every step, a lesson to be learned,
The hills we climb, the battles we have fought,
Are the fires in which our spirits are burned.

Yet, even in the darkest night,
There shines a light, unwavering and bright.
A beacon of hope, of faith, and grace,
Guiding us to our final resting place.
Through trials and tribulations, we walk on,
Knowing the path leads to the dawn.

You don't know my pain
We are not the same.
Try and see my view
I am not that her you once knew.
My thoughts of life have changed.

Now I See

Two years of my life was spent on foreign land.
I was serving my country, doing my duty at hand.

I was a wife and mother, with three children left at home.
Why was I leaving them behind; to venture into places unknown?

I didn't question "why" not really at that time,
For I knew there had to be a reason, somewhere deep within my mind.

All things work together for good...that's what the scriptures say
So there had to be some meaning for me to have to go so far away.

People were depending on me at home, in the Army, and at work.
How could I be all things to all of them and not feel like a jerk?

When you have been called upon to serve, your life is no longer your own.
I gave everything I had to ensure that those entrusted to my care would all return HOME.

My going to Afghanistan and Iraq was not just about the war.
It was a training ground for me to see things clearly on the home shore.

Pain

I never meant to hurt you
Yet that is all I seem to do
You only gave your love to me
As anyone could see,
The hurt is there
Deep within your heart
The pain has caused you to depart.
Why do we hurt the ones we love???
What a loss for both of us.
Will we ever learn to trust?
For though we have to change this love
I truly believed it came from up above.
The heavens smiled upon us
We met on levels yet untouched.
Others wonder what could it be
This love that surrounds you and me.
Love hurts sometimes.

Decision Making

The heart says - go for it.
The mind says - girl, you know better the spirit says - leave it alone.
So,
What do you do??
When
The heart is feeling
The mind is wondering
The spirit is speaking.
Do you answer the yearning that you feel? Do you listen to the words the mind is saying. Do you challenge yourself to test the spirit?
Weigh your options
Make a choice
Choose carefully
For much is at stake.

This Is Crazy Love

Insecurity stops the mouth from speaking what the heart is feeling
elevated above my conscience.
Too afraid to speak out - too many broken promises, to many wounds.
It is on my mind - cannot deny the gravitational pull of the heart. Once
the spirit speaks - what are we to do??
You have touched my inner person
Tapped into a quiet stillness which now wants to shout awakened the
still small voice of my poetic soul.
Will you listen as the voice cries out?
Will anyone want to hear how loudly the stillness speaks.
Are you telling me that i must stop this craziness.
We cannot help the way we feel.
The heart is racing at warp speed to a galactic atmospheric experience.
Come ride the stars with me to catch this magical dreamscape to
Venus.
Take a chance on this love.

Blue

From high above the clouds; sky blue
To the deep dark ocean floor sea
Turquoise shades to black
In-between the two on the surface it appears calm waters
Different shades of the persona
Light to dark
Happy to sad
Perception is one cool together sister.
Travel beneath the calm waters if you have time.
Search the deep dark recesses and discover
Hidden springs of wealth and warmth waiting to burst forth into the
heavens above.
Are you ready?
Are you sure you can handle it??

OMAN

Walk on The Beach.
I have lost myself in the gift of your love
Amazed and adrift on a secret sea.
Just you and me
Beneath the silver of the midnight sky
A tender embrace
A whisper
A sigh
Discovering treasures
We will have together
Today, tomorrow, now and forever.
I never really lived until I loved you.

Why do we hurt the ones we love???
What a loss for both of us.
Will we ever learn to trust?
For though we have to change this love
I truly believed it came from up above.
The heavens smiled upon us
We met on levels yet untouched. Others wonder what could it be this
love that surrounds you and me.
Love hurts sometimes.

At The Other End

You enter the tunnels of life, of love not knowing what to expect
All anxious wonderings abide within the crevices of the mind and
heart.
Unexplained feeling rise up from buried deep within the soul.
You are challenged by these thoughts
They bring tears, fears, secret wants, desires, untamed passions.
Yet
No one knows the torment you go through to hide these feeling to
keep these thoughts untold
You want to be able to come out on the other side
Fulfilled.

What Now

This is not what I was expecting nor looking for at this time;
Out of nowhere from the inside bringing forth beauty unseen.
The qualities are hidden from the natural,
But seen if you have the spiritual eye to look beyond the surface into
the Heart of the soul.
We look on the outside at the natural beauty;
Ebony brown skin, black flowing hair, pretty smile.
The body of a woman.
But
Beyond the skin, beneath the surface is what has now been brought to
my attention.
There is warmth, sincerity, caring, and true love.
It is seen in the way you carry yourself, the walk, your speech.
Your non-verbal communication speaks volumes to the listener.
I want to hear your every word.
Speak to me.
From now until eternity.
Let me hear your song; sing to me your sonata,
Play the melody which will soothe my very being.

Set Free

How do I begin to tell this truth?
When did the love stop???
It did not.
I still love you.
Compromising what I felt I needed so that we could continue as one.
I realized this was causing more harm than good.
The house, the car, the stuff
None of this matters more than me or you.
When all is said and done
Can you say that your are/were truly happy?
Do you even remember what happy feels like?
Real true happiness deep down in your soul happy. Happy to be your
true self.
I recall how that felt,
Free to be free
Childlike, unashamed, open, honest.
Does it mean I do not love you anymore?
No.
My love for you remains.
Am I still in love with you?
What has changed is my desire for more than compromise. Why did
you marry me?
Do you love me?
Are you still in love with me?
I have asked these questions before.
Can you answer truthfully?
The truth shall set you free.

The Potter's Hands

In the potter's hands, clay becomes art,
So are we shaped by life's unyielding test.
Each trial, each tribulation plays its part,
In molding us to become our best.
The wheel spins, the pressure applied,
Yet through it all, our spirit never breaks.
In every moment, God is by our side,
Guiding us through whatever path life takes.

This process of becoming, hard and long,
Is filled with pain, yet also with song.
For in our struggles, we find our true strength,
And in our faith, our hearts are stretched at length.
So, we embrace life's process, come what may,
Trusting in God to shape us, day by day.

The Seed's Journey

A seed, buried deep within the earth,
Faces darkness, solitude, and dearth.
Yet, within this confinement, it finds
A purpose, a call, as it unwinds.
Through soil and stone, it pushes, it strives,
A metaphor for our Christian lives.

Life's process, a journey of growth and pain,
Where loss often precedes the greatest gain.
Like the seed, we're buried, only to rise,
Reaching towards the ever-changing skies.
In faith, we grow, through trials, we're led,
Toward the light, by His word, we're fed.

This process of growth, of dying and living,
Teaches us the beauty of forgiving,
For as we break through the earth, reborn,
We find our true selves, no longer torn.
In God's garden, we flourish, we thrive,
In life's process, by grace, we survive.

SECTION 4

Back Home

The Quiet Return

In the silence of my room, I stand alone,
Where war's echoes fade to a distant drone.
Boots unlaced, from desert sands to my own floor,
A woman soldier, home, yet not as before.
I've seen horizons blaze and night skies bleed,
Fought for peace, sown courage, reaped valor's seed.
Now, amid familiar walls, I seek my peace,
In the warmth of home, my battle scars cease.

Echoes of Valor

Through the threshold, I step, a warrior's grace,
Leaving behind Afghanistan's relentless chase.
In my heart, a storm of memories reside,
Echoes of valor, where fear and bravery collide.
As a woman, I fought where many dared not tread,
Bearing arms, where only eagles dare to spread.
Now, back home, in the gentle embrace of night,
I find strength in the quiet, in the absence of fight.

Unseen Battles

I return, not with trophies, nor tales of glory,
But with a spirit tested, a personal story.
In the eyes of my kin, I search for understanding,
For I am a soldier, my experiences demanding.
Afghanistan's deserts, now miles and worlds away,
Yet the battles I fought, in my mind, still sway.
As a woman among warriors, I stood tall and proud,
Back home, I seek solace, away from the crowd.

The Warrior's Solace

Home, at last, the battlefield behind me lies,
Underneath these peaceful skies, my spirit flies.
As a woman in combat, I've seen life and death intertwine,
Now, seeking comfort in the old, familiar sign.
The laughter of friends, the touch of the breeze,
In these simple joys, my restless heart finds ease.
Afghanistan taught me of strength, of love, of loss,
Back home, I cherish peace, no matter the cost.

Return to Serenity

The journey back from war, a path of solitude,
In my return, I seek not applause, but quietude.
As a soldier, I've weathered storms, faced fears untold,
In Afghanistan's embrace, I found my resolve bold.
Now, in the sanctuary of home, I lay down my guard,
Reflecting on battles, both external and hard.
As a woman, as a warrior, I've played my part,
Back home, I heal, with hope in my heart.

The Pilgrim's Path

In this journey of faith, I walk the pilgrim's path,
Through valleys of shadow, facing trials and wrath.
Yet, in each step, I find His grace abound,
In every hardship, His love is found.
My armor, faith; my shield, His word,
Against life's battles, His promises heard.
As a Christian, I tread, not in solitude, but in light,
Guided by His truth, by His might.

The Builder's Faith

As a builder in this world, I lay each stone with care,
Foundation in Christ, in His love, I share.
With every brick, a testament of faith,
In the face of storms, His strength I embrace.
This house I build, not on sand, but rock,
Against the floods, it shall stand, withstand the shock.
In this life's construction, His word my guide,
In Him, I find my place, in Him, I reside.

FROM MY HEART

Side by side in bed we lay
So close, yet still we are far away.
I sure do miss your loving touch
My body aches for oh so much.
Where has it gone?
Is it that you no longer care?
Did my body changes cause you to stare?
Has your love been filled elsewhere?
The Cancer; You know was not my fault.
The surgeries; the pain; the weak and tired days I've spent.
I'm Still Fighting!!!
The vows we took said "till death do us part".
Well;
You should know,
This is killing me.

My cancer journey
It started as a little dot, an image on the X-ray screen.
It ended with a Mastectomy.

The Gardener's Trust

In the garden of life, I sow with hope,
In the soil of faith, I find my scope.
Each seed, a prayer, in trust, I lay,
Under His sun, they grow, by night, by day.
Thorns may rise, yet flowers bloom,
In His grace, even through gloom.
As a gardener, in His love, I trust,
For in His garden, we grow, we must.

BACK HOME

My cancer journey
It started as a little dot, an image on the X-ray screen.
It ended with a Mastectomy.

I would hope that the weight of love in your heart outweighs the extra
weight now around my waist.

SECTION 5

No Words

Beyond Words

In the silence that follows the storm,
Where echoes of battle grow faint and forlorn,
I stand amidst the calm, yet inside I roar,
A woman soldier with stories that words can't explore.
The sights I've seen, the pain I've known,
Lie beyond the reach where words have flown.
In this quietude, my spirit seeks
A solace that silence, in whispers, speaks.

The Unspoken Return

I've returned from lands where speech falls short,
Where actions speak and battles are fought.
As a woman among warriors, I've held my ground,
In the realm of the speechless, my voice I found.
Now, back home, words fail to convey
The depth of the journey, the price I've paid.
In the gaze of those who welcome me back,
I search for understanding, where language lacks.

Silence After War

The battlefield's clamor now lies behind,
Leaving a silence of a different kind.
As a soldier, words were my unseen shield,
Now, back home, my lips are sealed.
The stories I carry, too heavy for words,
Like the weightless flight of returning birds.
In my heart, a quiet peace tries to grow,
Amidst the speechless memories of long ago.

The Quiet Warrior

Home at last, where words should flow,
Yet, I find myself caught in the undertow.
Of a silent struggle, a speechless fight,
Where memories of war turn day into night.
As a woman who stood on Afghanistan's sands,
I've come back with empty hands.
Hands that can't convey or write
The depth of the darkness or the value of the light.

Echoes of the Voiceless

In the aftermath, where voices fade,
My experiences in shadows, silently laid.
No words to express, no tales to tell,
Just a heart beating a silent knell.
The war may be over, the battle done,
But the speechless journey has just begun.
As a woman, a soldier, I've seen what's unsaid,
In the land of the speechless, I've fearlessly tread.

War

This war on terrorism is real
They do not care who they hurt or kill.
The towers fell, fears assailed
All hope is not lost.
We will fight to pay the cost.
We will not give up.
Osama, Saddam,
Al-Qaeda, Taliban
Whomever,
September 11th
America will always remember.
The war continues.

Is it crazy???
Yes it is.

The Silent Prayer

In the quiet of my soul, where words disappear,
I find a prayer too deep, too sincere.
For the language of faith needs no sound,
In the heart of the believer, it's profoundly found.
As a Christian, my spirit speaks without voice,
In the silent communion, I rejoice.
For even in silence, His presence I feel,
In the wordless moments, His love is real.

You have not because you ask not
What is it that you want?
Cannot seem to grasp it.
Don't have enough money?
If you could buy it, you'd have it. Possessions.
The things you want are not necessarily the things you need.
Your heavenly father already knows what you have need of. He is rich
beyond your imagination.
Just ask and you shall receive.

Speechless Before the Divine

Before Your majesty, my words fall short,
In the awe of Your presence, my thoughts contort.
As a Christian, I stand, humbled and mute,
For no words can match Your attributes absolute.
In the silent adoration of Your grace,
I find my refuge, my holy place.
Without words, my soul sings Your praise,
In the speechless awe, my hands I raise.

Epithet

You are the unexplained conclusion to the question.
Others see the sensual, sexual, muscular being that you are.
Yet, for me; your beauty is that your presence exudes your love
towards me.
I see you as the prototype. The model from which this present
generation could learn from.
Home groomed. Grandma, mother, sisters; no brother.
Strong black female persuasion.
Leading you towards your tomorrows.
Respectful.
Giving back through your written/spoken word. Teaching others what
you already know.
Your reality through your spirituality,
May you continue to bless us. My brother.
Thank you.

The Wordless Witness

In a world clamoring for a voice,
I find my strength in a quieter choice.
As a Christian, my faith is silently shown,
Not in words, but in love alone.
For when words are insufficient to convey,
The acts of faith speak in a profound way.
In the speechless journey of my soul's quest,
I find Your love, and in Your love, I rest.

I Miss

Children's laughter
Bubble baths
Familiar faces and places
Green grass
Rain showers, thunderstorms
Hot cooked meals
Making love
Shopping malls
Pizza, subway, burger king
Dogs barking
Rush hour traffic
Ice cream
The Tom Joyner morning radio show
Co-workers
Driving my vehicle.
Just a few of the little things
Amazing what comes to mind when all you have is time.

No Words

Reflections of me "v"
I remember your smile daddy.
But, at the age of five you were gone.
Not until I was grown did I fully understand.
As a child, teased, hurt, misunderstood.
I ran a lot from age nine to sixteen. Elementary school to senior high.
Never really thought about why.
I loved the freedom.
As I look back now I see
It was an escape from pain, people, life.
On the track I could win - just me and the wind,
Overprotected. Yes, but never neglected,
Mom did an exceptional job.
Well educated. We all went to college. Nothing less was expected.
Looking for love, marriage, children.
Did I fall to fast. Settled for love or a
Mirror of happiness.
Compromises.
Learning to love.
Be careful what you ask for.
Now, mom is gone too,.
Expectations of others, guiding which road to travel no longer exists.
God is the only judge.
The paths traveled to reach this point all had purpose.
The road ahead is open for exploration.
Are you moving towards the possibilities unlimited?
Or
Staying on the road less traveled.
Stagnated
Diamond girl
Dedicated to the female first sergeant

FROM MY HEART

All the signs are evident
It is a mans world
No matter what you do
Someone is forever watching you.
You strive to be the best
That is what the advertisements say
Jealousy, envy, strife
They all climb the ladder with you along the way.
Stripes
These stripes of mine were earned
There were roadblocks at every turn
Criticism, ostracism,
Off limits to certain arenas.
The rise to the top
Had many hurdles to overcome.
From private to first sergeant.

Destiny cannot be stopped the pinnacle of excellence
The top.

No man knows the hour or the day today your soul could be required.

A New Life Found In Following Christ

Battlegrounds to Blessings

In the dust of Afghanistan, where shadows dance with light,
A warrior stood, her armor worn, amidst the endless fight.
Yet in her heart, a different call began to stir and rise,
A consecration, deep and true, beneath those war-torn skies.

No longer just a soldier in the battles of the land,
But now a warrior for Christ, with faith as her command.
Her scars, the marks of battles past, now symbols of His grace,
Each one a story of the love that found her in that place.

From gunfire to the Gospel, she walks a path so bold,
Her heart consecrated, in His mighty fold.
The battlefield has changed, but the fight remains as real,
With the armor of God, her spirit does heal.

From Desert Sands to Living Waters

Amidst the arid desert lands, a soldier's journey grew,
Against the backdrop of the war, a different battle knew.
From the sands of strife and sorrow, to the living waters clear,
She found her consecration, as she drew to Jesus near.

Her hands, once poised for combat, now raised in prayer and praise,
Her heart, once guarded fiercely, now open in His gaze.
For in the silence of the desert, His voice became her guide,
Leading her from conflict's chaos, to be by His side.

In the consecration of her spirit, she found a peace so sweet,
A soldier now in Christ's own army, her mission to complete.
The desert blooms around her, where once there was just sand,
For she walks in living waters, with her Savior hand in hand.

Armor of Faith

She bore the weight of armor, in lands so far from home,
Fighting not just for country, but for every place she'd roam.
Yet amidst the clash and clamor, a different call she heard,
A consecration of her soul, moved by God's living Word.

Her battle scars are many, her stories deep and vast,
But in the shadow of the Cross, her lot is cast.
She trades her earthly armor for the armor of her faith,
Following Christ with every step, in every breath she takes.

Her journey speaks of transformation, from soldier to the saved,
Her life a testament to the power of the grace she craved.
Consecrated, now she marches, not to war, but peace,
Her mission to proclaim His love, till all conflicts cease.

Warrior's Witness

From Kabul's rugged mountains to the valleys of Kandahar,
She served with honor, strength, and pride, beneath the evening star.
But now her heart belongs to Him who reigns above all lands,
Her consecration complete, her life in His hands.

The battlefield of faith is where she now engages fight,
With the Gospel as her weapon, and His truth her light.
Her testimony powerful, a beacon to the lost,
A reminder of the price of freedom, and the cost.

She follows Christ with fervor, a warrior still at heart,
Her past a foundation, from which she'll never part.
Consecrated, dedicated, to her Lord above,
She serves now with a different strength, propelled by His love.

Peace in the Aftermath

Once a soldier in the dust, where echoes of war resound,
Now a follower of Christ, where true peace is found.
Her consecration not just a moment, but a journey wide and deep,
A promise to her Savior, a vow she'll always keep.

In the stillness of the morning, in the quiet of the night,
She feels His presence with her, turning darkness into light.
Her life, a living sacrifice, to God who guides her way,
From the battlegrounds to blessings, in His grace, she'll stay.

The Shepherd's Call

In the garden of my heart, where thorns and thistles grow,
The Shepherd called my name, in a voice soft and low.
He led me through the valleys, where shadows loom so large,
Consecrating my journey, as He took charge.

His rod and staff, my comfort, in the trials that I face,
Following Him, I find my stride, empowered by His grace.
The path may twist and turn, but His direction is my guide,
In the consecration of my soul, in His love, I abide.

Lord God.

Continue to speak to me.
Show me what you want me to see,
Tell me what you want me to say.
It's all about knowing your way.,
No, I am not a Preacher.
But, we all are called to minister.
To tend to the needs of others.
To show true love towards our sisters and brothers.
AGAPE Love is Easy;
When you follow Christ.

Why

Why can't I tell them, why can't I share?
How I really feel inside, how much I really do care.
For they are my heart. My family,
Yet, I know they don't know the whole story.
Will they ever get to hear it all?
One day,
Just;
Not from me.

LORD,
Open my eyes,
Open my ears,
Open my mouth,
Open my heart.

That I may see clearly past the distractions.
That I may hear your still small voice, even in the noise.
That I may speak your truths not man's feelings.
So, that your LOVE is felt.
This is my prayer.

Consecrate me Lord.
To thy service.
For your service.
For the world.
Use me to do your work and your will.

What I think of as a delay,
Could actually be that there is something, someone, or maybe even me
That God is using to further His progress.
My job is to Praise HIM through the process.
The delay could be God working out the details,
Moving the obstacles and opening the doors.
Wait on the Lord.

Choose

Follow your family's dysfunction.
Follow your friend's destruction.
Follow in someone else's footsteps.
Or
Make up your mind and
Follow Christ.

Home

There is a saying that "Home is where the heart is".
That may not always be a cozy, warm, friendly place.
I think it's where you feel the most comfortable with yourself.
A soldier's home could be a tent, the ground, a bunk, or a sleeping bag.
Returning from the battlefield requires an adjustment of the mind.
You are expected to fall back into the daily routines of family life.
As a wife, and mother you are supposed to perform your household duties.
I just came back from a war zone; a hostile environment, a not so friendly place.
Do you think I can just fall back into daily regular cooking and cleaning and having sex.
That has not been my life for almost two years.
YES
I want intimacy but I don't want to be touched.
I want conversation, but I don't want to talk.
I miss you all, but I don't want to be around you.
I know it doesn't make sense.
Peace, for me, is found sitting alone in the quietness wherever I can find it.
No mortar rounds, not bullets flying, no diesel engine smells, not fire pits.
I cannot apologize enough.
I don't want to argue.
BUT, you just don't understand.

There is no room for me or I, because of HE.
HE who is King.

The Lord is in the Temple, let everybody bow.
HIS train fills the temple.
This means that when I am in that place of reverence and worship there is
Nothing more important than my love for HIM.
HE is All and HE deserves my all.

With all of the planning, plotting, and waiting for my downfall to happen;
What you should have been doing was asking me why it never took place.

God's timing is eternal.
Stop wasting your "now" time before it comes to an end.
Use what time you have to make a difference.

Kingdom business is not about the academic, but the Apostolic.
You need to know the word of God.
But the world needs to see you live the word of God that you know.

Fog

From a distance the fog appears to cover a lot of space.
Problems may appear to be insurmountable for you.
But if you keep moving forward towards the goal, you will see that the
sun is burning off the fog.

You can now walk on dry ground.
Jesus, the Son of God has made it possible for us to walk through this
life and all of the problems we may face.
Accept HIM and trust HIM with your life.

Your mind is a strategic planning battlefield.
You can train, read your manual (God's word); get equipped and survive.
Or,
You can go out unprepared and die.
The battle is not yours.
The victory is already won.
You must fight with faith.

If you want to know if a friend is shallow; find out how far out into the deep they will go with you.

If you are out in the deep waters and they stay on the shore, you just might drown.

You see the clouds, so you expect the rain.
I see the rainbow and anticipate the sun.
It's all in perspective.
Don't let the clouds keep you from seeing the rainbow.
Look beyond the circumstances of your life which may have you feeling weighed down.
Continue and chase your dreams.
Just like the dark clouds will eventually move on; so will this season in your life.
The sun is shining just behind the clouds.

There is a storm coming in your life that you need to be prepared for.
There are warnings ahead of time that you may have ignored.
Excuses will not save you. Only a relationship with Jesus will.
We take so much for granted.
Life is short.
Make it count.

The blades on the fan are spinning fast.
Life sometimes may feel the same.
Things may seem like they are out of control.
They are not.
Take a step back and look up.
The fan has a cord which controls how fast the blades spin.
Pull the cord, and the blades slow down.
Pull it again, and the fan comes to a stop.
Look at your life and pull the cord on whatever is spinning you out of control.
Slow down the downward spiral.
Take back the control.
You have the power.

New month. New Week. New Day. New Beginnings.
Same You equals No changes.
There has to be an indication of the transformation.
The saints of old used to say "you ought to show some sign."
You can't just sing and say I know I've been changed.
Where is the proof?
Is your light on and shining in the dark places?
You have to want to change.
Only then will the processing begin to take place.
Don't quit when it gets hard.
Work through it and get your Victory.

A branch of the tree can be broken and barely hanging on.
BUT,
It is still connected to the tree. The tree is still rooted in fertile soil.
You may feel defeated, deflated, despised, or denied at times.
BUT,
If you are connected to Jesus Christ, the true vine.
I can guarantee that you have a solid foundation on which you can stand.
No matter what tries to knock you down or cut you off.
Hold fast to your faith, and you will survive.

We all have some scars.

Some of us have been bruised or battered by life's circumstances.

Your lumps and scars might be larger or smaller than mine.

You may have healed from your bruises so no one even knows that you had any.

Well,

If you know Jesus in the pardon of your sins, you have been inspected and approved.

You no longer need to feel ashamed.

Walk in your power and sweet victory.

Let the world know that you are free.

If you find obstacles in your way.
Make a decision.
Go through it; go around it; take another route or make a new path.
Just don't go backwards.
Find a way to keep moving forward.

Endurance

Can you keep your faith and stay in the race until the end.
No matter what that end may be.
Because even though the battle has been fought and Victory has
already been won through Jesus Christ and his sacrifice.
You still have to fight.
Fight your fears, your flesh, and your doubts.

The rain will wet you
The shower/bath will rinse you
The soap will fragrance you
BUT
When you are washed in the blood, you will be cleansed of all
unrighteousness.

As a soldier in the Army of the Lord we have discharge orders.
We are to "go ye therefore into all nations...
We are on a mission.
We must always be ready to serve.
Our mind, shield, sword, and weapons should be clean and loaded for warfare.
You never know when your next call to action will be.
Service is an attitude.
You have to be willing, no matter the outcome.
We go to battle, but the victory has already been won.
Just keep showing up.
God honors faithfulness.

ABOUT THE AUTHOR

Valencia Davis, a Florida native, has lived a life woven into an inspiring tapestry of resilience, dedication, and artistic expression. A survivor in every sense, Valencia triumphed over breast cancer, a battle that shaped her into the embodiment of perseverance. With over 30 years of service as a social worker, she devoted her life to helping others, leaving an indelible mark on the lives she touched. Her commitment extended to the military, where she served as a retired Sgt 1st Class in the US Army for over two decades, demonstrating not only her dedication to her country but also her unwavering strength.

A pillar of enduring love, Valencia has been happily married to her husband, Jack, for an incredible 36 years. Together, they have raised three wonderful adult children, Bryan, Faith, and James, forming a close-knit family that embodies the values of love, resilience, and unity.

Rooted in her unwavering faith, Valencia finds solace and inspiration in Psalm 91, a verse that graces her mornings and nights with a profound sense of purpose. Her love for God is the cornerstone of her existence, and she places her faith above all else, navigating life's challenges with grace and conviction.

From the corridors of senior high school, Valencia discovered her passion for poetry, a form of expression that allowed her to convey the depth of her emotions and thoughts. Inspired by literary giants such as Nikki Giovanni and Maya Angelou, she embarked on a poetic journey that would become a lifelong companion. Poetry is a medium where individuals can uniquely articulate their feelings and thoughts. Whether through screenplays or verses, writing has been her sanctuary, providing an outlet for self-expression and a canvas for her creative spirit to flourish.

What sets Valencia's poetry apart is the backdrop against which much of it was penned – while serving overseas in the armed forces. The verses carry the echoes of distant lands, reflecting not only her personal experiences but also the universality of emotions that transcend borders.

In "From My Heart", readers are invited to delve into a world where resilience meets creativity, faith intertwines with expression, and the journey unfolds through the artistry of words. Valencia is available for corporate book signings, events and appearances.

For Bulk Inquiries please contact:
Support@buildabrother.com
Build A Brother Publishing

Made in the USA
Columbia, SC
11 April 2024

34124488R00072